Contemporary Crafts

Gilding & Lacquering

RODRIGO & ROSARIA TITIAN

Contemporary Crafts

Gilding & Lacquering

RODRIGO & ROSARIA TITIAN

An Owl Book

HENRY HOLT
AND
COMPANY

NEW YORK

THE AUTHORS

Rodrigo and Rosaria Titian have been restorers all their
working lives; they run a busy studio established in 1963 by
Rodrigo's father, Salvatore. Rosaria specializes in lacquer
restoration and painted furniture while Rodrigo concentrates
on the areas of carving, gilding and cabinet work. In addition
to their restoration work, they teach a number of courses in
gilding and painted finishes.

Henry Holt and Company, Inc.
Publishers since 1866
115 West 18th Street
New York, New York 10011

Henry Holt® is a registered
trademark of Henry Holt and Company, Inc.

Library of Congress Catalog Card Number:
94-76065

ISBN 0-8050-3325-4

Henry Holt books are available for special promotions and premiums.
For details contact: Director, Special Markets.

First American/Owl Book Edition—1994

Designed and edited by Anness Publishing Limited, London
Editorial Director: Joanna Lorenz
Editor: Penelope Cream
Art Director: Tony Paine
Designer: Roy Prescott
Photographer: Tony Buckley

Printed and bound in Spain

1 3 5 7 9 10 8 6 4 2

CONTENTS

INTRODUCTION

GILDING

The origins of the art of gilding date back to the Sumerians and the Egyptians some 3,500 years ago. They discovered that gold could be beaten into thin sheets and then applied to surfaces. There are records that show that the Chinese, Greek and Roman civilizations also used gilding to embellish their work, ranging from furniture and ornaments to architecture. During the Middle Ages the use of gold was confined to Asia and the Middle East. In Europe it was not until the fourteenth century that gilding was used again, applied to icons and other ecclesiastical works.

It was Cennino Cennini, in his book *Il Libro Dell'Arte* published in 1437, who first brought the art of gilding to the hands of the ordinary layman. Cennini is quoted as writing that this book was 'made and composed by Cennini of Colle for the use and good profit of anyone who wants to enter this profession'. Cennini, himself a craftsman whose tutor trained directly under Giotto, gives an exceptionally detailed analysis of the processes involved in both water and oil gilding.

Artists such as Giotto, Duccio and Masaccio in their religious works on triptychs and icons furthered the process on gilding by discovering that the wood, which was porous, had to be covered with gesso so that the gold would not flake off. Gesso was applied to seal the wood, but was still not good enough because it was water porous. The

.... *A nineteenth-century Chinese export lacquer linen press with gold decoration.*

uses of natural clay were adapted and applied, and because of its water-repellent properties it was the ideal ally to gesso. Apart from accepting the gold much more easily it also helped to give it greater depth and colour.

To apply the gold, a leaf was put on a padded leather cushion which, unlike today, had no parchment border around one side. It was then blown flat and cut to size with a gilder's knife. The gold was picked up on a piece of card, using static from the gilder's hair to make it adhere. Nowadays a gilder's tip is used which has long soft hairs (usually squirrel) set between two pieces of card. Water mixed with size and spirit (alcohol) was applied to the clay - hence the expression 'water gilding' - and once the gold came into contact with the wet surface it was sucked onto it like a magnet. When the gold had been applied it was burnished to give it a strong metallic look. This was originally done with a dog's tooth until the stone agate was found and refined. The agate was polished smooth and mounted on a wooden handle. When passed over the surface of the gilded piece a number of times it brought out the natural shine and brilliance of the gold and also made it adhere further to the decorated surface.

Gold used to be beaten into thin sheets by hammering it between layers of sheepskin and ox intestines on stone slabs to absorb the shocks and vibrations. Nowadays it is beaten between hydraulic presses and can be produced to a thickness of 0.0001 mm thick; it is then cut into small squares.

The colour of gold leaf depends a great deal on its purity; the higher the carat the more brilliant the

gold looks, the lower the carat the more impurities (other metals) it has in it. It also comes in various shades ranging from greens to yellows to orange according to the alloys such as silver and copper employed in the beating. A technique documented in Cennini's book was to use silver leaf rather than gold leaf for cost efficiency, and then cover it with a yellow tinted varnish to give the impression of it being a high carat gold. Silver was also used in its own right by certain masters for very specific illusionistic purposes.

Oriental cabinets brought into Europe around the middle of the seventeenth century required stands which were lavishly gilded in either silver or gold. As techniques progressed, craftsmen became bolder in their designs and workmanship became more complex. Cabinets were made for the European market by local craftsmen who imitated lacquer by using shellac. The gold motifs and designs were applied by using oil gilding or, as it is sometimes described, mordant gilding; this process involves the use of a sticky size. Cennini described his oil size as being made of linseed oil, which was either boiled or left out in the sun to dry it slightly to make it thicker. Some used varnish and lead white or verdigris (a green crystallized substance formed on copper when it ages) to act as drying agents. Once tacky, the gold was applied on top (nowadays ready-mixed oil sizes are easily available).

Sometimes a gold paint would have been used for extremely fine decoration; this was made by grinding gold leaf with egg white and was known as shell gold, so called because it was usually kept in a mussel or similar shell. Especially in England, during the reign of Queen Anne (1702-1714), many gilt tables and chairs featured very high-quality foliate designs in low relief carving in gesso. These were probably made for state banquet rooms for display use only.

Gilding on glass was a popular technique used to enhance mirror edges and borders. The gold would be applied (using water gilding techniques for laying only) to the reverse of the glass, and would then be left to dry. A design was scratched out using a blunt instrument, such as a sharp wooden dowel; once completed it would quite often be given a backing colour which would protect the gold from being scratched. It would also help to enhance the detail of the design. This technique is known as 'verre églomisé'.

Currently there are many different forms of leaf, ranging from platinum, palladium, silver, white gold, aluminium and metal or schlag (composition) leaf. There are even paillons of gold and silver which are much thicker leaves than normal, up to four times the thickness of an ordinary sheet, and also sprays and cellulose paints. All these have their own look and charm, but none will ever have the depth, brilliance and aesthetically magnetic attraction of gold itself.

LACQUERING

The art of lacquer originated more than a thousand years ago; although an accurate date has never been established, archaeologists' discoveries suggest that wooden objects from the first millenium BC in China were covered with a substance believed to be the sap of *Rhus Verniciflua* tree. The Chinese name for lacquer was 'urushi', and it became known as 'lacquer' by the Europeans. This substance is now known as 'true lacquer'.

The *Rhus Verniciflua* tree was indigenous to China although the craft of lacquering flourished throughout the east coast of Asia, particularly in Japan and Korea. One reason for this was the emigration of craftsmen during the violent wars of the years 481-221 BC, known as the 'warring states period'. It appears that the Chinese introduced this art form to the Japanese through Korea as well as the seeds of the *Rhus Verniciflua* tree for planting.

The production of lacquer was a long and tedious exercise, the extraction of the sap never changing over the centuries. Thankfully this extraction did not kill the trees, but the handling of the raw lacquer caused skin diseases for it was highly toxic; buying and treating the raw material was usually left to the assistants because the artists and craftsmen were regarded as too important to risk harming.

The sap was extracted by cutting horizontally into the bark and small copper cups were tied under the cuts to collect the resin or latex. The thick transparent sap turned dark brown or black on exposure to the air. It was then filtered through

*An early nineteenth-century Neapolitan chair
with striking arm supports, decorated in
both paint and gilt.*

. . . .

a hempen cloth to remove impurities and slowly boiled to give an even consistency and to evaporate superfluous moisture. The surface was prepared by filling cracks and holes with a rice paste and lacquer mixture. The layers of lacquer were then applied in very thin coats and allowed to dry in a moist atmosphere. Different coloured pigments were applied between coats to give the different coloured lacquers – a similar process to that used today. Some incised lacquers can have up to 300 coats, each layer being rubbed smooth with fine charcoal dust and 'horn ash'. The lacquer was then decorated with various gold dust and metals or painted with scenes of figures and animals or birds.

Resin lac, or shellac, is a greeny substance deposited on the branches of trees by the insect Coccus Lacca which feeds on the sap. The resin is obtained either by scraping the branches or by taking the whole twig. Once collected it is then slowly heated and sieved to remove any waste. While it is still hot it is spread into thin layers and left to dry. Once dry it is broken up into small flakes and stored. Shellac was originally used extensively in Islamic countries especially on buildings and interiors to protect the wood from damp and rot. It was also used on furniture.

The use of shellac varnish preceded the appearance of oriental lacquer in Europe. The Dutch and East Indian Companies imported such decorated furniture, and, once the fashion had spread, the increased demand for lacquered and oriental furniture meant that European designs and models were sent to the East to enable craftsmen there to produce lacquered furniture for European requirements. It was not long before European cabinet makers were producing imitations of oriental lacquer. This became known as japanning.

The seventeenth and eighteenth centuries saw a boom for japanning which led to many workshops all over Europe creating their own recipes. This style involved the wooden foundation being painted with several coats of gesso and size which, when dry, were rubbed smooth as close to the wood as possible to fill the grain. The surface was then given a few coats of thick seed lac varnish mixed with powder pigments of varying colours, left to dry and rubbed down to a very smooth finish. Gold and silver leaf and gold, silver and bronze powders were applied by means of gold size, and inkwork on the designs to define and create a scene. Over 10 coats of seed lac varnish covered the surface. When it was dry it was polished with cork and rottenstone. This technique was adapted and later applied to papier-mâché, and to metal in a style known as toleware.

Urushi (lacquer) shellac is still used today. However, man-made substitutes which are cheaper and less time-consuming to apply have replaced many of the traditional techniques, although there are many skilled craftsmen and women still using original methods and materials. As cost-effective as these modern materials may be, the durability and deep, lustrous colours of true lacquer remain unsurpassed.

MATERIALS AND EQUIPMENT

THE MATERIALS and equipment required for gilding and lacquering are readily available, although some of the supplies may be found more easily in specialist gilding shops or artists' suppliers.

WHITE (MINERAL) SPIRIT
This is an oil-based solvent which can be used to dilute oil-based varnishes and colours. It is also useful for washing out brushes after use with oil-based paints.

METHYLATED SPIRIT (WOOD ALCOHOL)
This is used to clean brushes after applications of polish. It is also a diluting agent for gilding water.

GILDING WATER
This liquid is used to attach loose leaf gold or silver in water gilding. It is mixed from cold water, methylated spirit (wood alcohol) and heated rabbit-skin size.

CHALK PASTELS
These are available in a variety of colours and are useful for transferring a traced design onto a surface to be decorated. For ease of visibility, it is best to use pale colours for designs on a dark background, and deep colours on a light background.

OIL COLOURS
The price of oil colours varies according to their quality. Students' colours tend to be cheaper than artists' colours, although the colour may not be as good and they may fade more quickly. However,

they are a good alternative to artists' colours if these are not available. Always dilute oil colours with varnish and white (mineral) spirit before applying them to furniture.

WATER COLOURS
For most effective results, buy these paints by the tube as they tend to be of better quality. Mix water colours into clay solutions and water-based size to alter the shade. Gouache paints can also be used with similar results.

BRUSHES
SABLE BRUSHES: these are relatively expensive brushes but are excellent for painting details and inking intricate designs. When selecting a brush, make sure it has a good point. Clean the brushes immediately after use. Good synthetic brushes are now available and can be used as a cheaper and less delicate alternative to sable.

BRISTLE BRUSHES: these are relatively cheap, hard-wearing, multi-purpose brushes, useful for applying paints and varnishes. Collect a variety of sizes for different areas, and ensure they are clean and dry before use.

STENCIL BRUSHES: these short, stubby, hair brushes, normally used for painting stencilled designs, are excellent for applying transfer gold or silver. Make sure they are clean and dry before use.

HOG BRUSHES: these come in various sizes and are

either flat or round-headed. They are used for mixing clay colours and also for applying yellow clay (red clay is applied using a sable brush).

BADGER BRUSHES: these are fairly expensive brushes, and are used for softening varnish to remove any visible lines. This type of brush must be cleaned very carefully after use by wiping it gently on a soft rag soaked in white (mineral) spirit. It should then be washed in warm soapy water and rinsed in clean water. Shake out any remaining water to make the bristles fluffy.

SOFT RAGS

Cotton rags are the most suitable for use in gilding and lacquering projects and can be easily torn from old sheets or pillowcases. Take care to avoid woollen rags as these collect too much dust and so are not a good choice for cleaning a surface before painting or varnishing.

SANDPAPER

'Wet or dry' sandpaper is best for use on pieces of furniture or other objects to be decorated, and can be used either with water or dry. Different grades are available and determine the coarseness of the grain. Silicone carbide sandpaper is good for sharpening gilding knives, and for sanding down between coats of paint or varnish.

INDIAN INK

This is a dense ink used to outline designs or add details to a decoration. It is best applied with a fine-pointed sable brush. Some types of Indian ink contain polish and dry very quickly. Other varieties do not have any polish and this makes it easier to wipe off any mistakes while still wet. Ink without polish needs fixing before varnishing or it will run and the design will be spoilt.

EGGSHELL (SEMI-GLOSS) PAINT

This is an oil-based paint which is applied on top of an undercoat. The paint does not cover the surface as well, but leaves it smooth and hard, ready to take glazes and oil colour. White (mineral) spirit can be used to thin eggshell paint and to clean brushes after application.

UNDERCOAT

An oil-based undercoat paint should be used as a first coat on an object. It acts as a primer on wood and provides a working surface for subsequent layers. Undercoats tend to vary so always refer to the manufacturer's instructions as to application and drying times.

RED OXIDE METAL PRIMER

This should be applied as a first coat before applying paint to metal. It prevents the metal from rusting and allows further coats of paint to adhere better, which, in turn, avoids the possibility of scratching and flaking. Refer to the manufacturer's instructions for exact details of use as each type of metal primer is slightly different.

GLOSS VARNISH

It is important to use a good-quality gloss varnish when sealing a pale-coloured surface. Avoid heavy-duty varnishes such as yacht varnish as this tends to dry with a heavy finish and will eventually turn yellow. Polyurethane varnishes come in various finishes including gloss, eggshell and matt. To add a tint to varnish, mix in a small amount of oil colour. After varnishing, always clean brushes in white (mineral) spirit.

T-CUT

This is an abrasive liquid that is used to smooth varnish and help reduce the dust on the surface. It will produce a pleasant, slightly matt finish on pieces and can be used where a very glossy result is not required.

BURNISHING CREAM

This is a cream similar to T-cut although slightly less abrasive.

POLISH (SHELLAC)

Polish (shellac) comes in a variety of types suitable for different applications; these include button polish, white polish and transparent polish. Any of these can be used to fix gold, but remember that they vary slightly in colour when applied. Use methylated spirit (wood alcohol) to thin polish and to clean brushes after application. Polish dries very quickly so be sure to read the manufacturer's instructions before use.

PAINT STRIPPER

This can be used to strip old paint and varnish from small pieces of furniture before decoration is applied. Always wear protective gloves and a mask and only use the stripper in a well-ventilated place, and preferably outside. If the piece of furniture is large it is worth considering having it stripped by a professional firm. This may well involve dipping the piece in caustic soda so it will need neutralizing with vinegar before applying gesso.

FILLER

Ready-mixed filler can be used to fill holes and dents in furniture or wooden objects. It dries to form a hard surface but is not as smooth as putty filler since it is more porous.

GESSO

Gesso, or whiting, is a chalk powder, used as the base for producing gesso solution, the first coat of gesso and putty. Ready-mixed acrylic gesso is also available.

RABBIT-SKIN SIZE GRANULES

Rabbit-skin size is used to produce the solution for gesso, putty, clay colours and gilding water.

WAX

Wax can be applied to objects to protect decorative features and can change their appearance slightly. Clear wax or beeswax can be rubbed onto carvings or mouldings and then covered in rottenstone to achieve an antique effect. Coloured waxes will produce the same effect but with a different finish.

ROTTENSTONE

This is a stone-coloured powder that is used to produce an antique finish. It is usually applied to mouldings or carvings and sticks to waxed surfaces.

AGATE BURNISHER

This is a small piece of agate stone mounted in a handle; is rubbed over water gilded leaf to give a high shine.

OIL COLOURS

BRISTLE BRUSHES

BADGER BRUSH

INDIAN INK

CHALK PASTELS

SABLE BRUSHES

PENCIL

TRACING PAPER

TRANSPARENT POLISH (SHELLAC)

GLOSS VARNISH

PAINT STRIPPER

BURNISHING CREAM

RED OXIDE METAL PRIMER

STEEL WOOL

GREEN UNDERCOAT

READY-MIXED FILLER

WHITE (MINERAL) SPIRIT

SPATULAS

WET AND DRY SANDPAPER

WHITE EGGSHELL (SEMI-GLOSS) PAINT

CLEAR WAX

T-CUT

STENCIL BRUSHES

GESSO (PUTTY)

WOOD GLUE

BLACK EGGSHELL (SEMI-GLOSS) PAINT

GILDER'S PAD, KNIFE AND TIP

These are used together to lay loose leaf. The leaf is laid on a soft pad (surrounded by a parchment or paper screen to shield against draughts), and, if necessary, is cut using the knife. A round-ended kitchen knife can be used if it is free from nicks in the blade. The tip, a soft, wide brush, is used to pick up the leaf and lay it on the surface to be decorated. Petroleum jelly may be used to add extra adherence to the tip.

GOLD LEAF

This comes in 2 forms: loose leaf or transfer. Both types are purchased in books containing 25 leaves, and measure 80 cm x 80 cm (32 in x 32 in). Loose leaf books contain loose sheets of thinly-beaten gold. Loose leaf gold is applied using a gilder's pad, knife and tip. Transfer gold is also beaten but is pressed onto waxed paper. It is applied using the thumb or a stencil brush. Gold leaf is available in many different shades; its carat may vary.

SILVER LEAF, YELLOW GOLD AND ALUMINIUM LEAF

These are all derivatives of gold, with other metals added. They are available in both loose leaf and transfer form.

SCHLAG (COMPOSITION) LEAF

This leaf is produced from a combination of all the impurities from all the different types of leaf put together. It resembles gold leaf but is cheaper.

LIQUID LEAF

This is a combination of red primer and metallic particles. It can be applied to metal, wood and plaster and comes in various shades. Remember to shake the bottle well before use.

BRONZE, ALUMINIUM AND SILVER POWDERS

These are mixed with varnish or polish (shellac) or applied to size, and are used to colour designs.

WATER-BASED SIZE

This is a rapidly drying synthetic size which becomes tacky after 15 minutes. It is ideal for quick oil gilding but is not as shiny as oil-based size.

GILDER'S PAD

GILDER'S TIP

SILVER LEAF

GILDER'S KN

YELLOW GOLD

ALUMINIUM LEAF

SCHLAG (COMPOSITION) LEAF

COTTON WOOL (COTTON BALLS)

LO

SILVER TRANSFER LEAF

OIL-BASED SIZE

This is available as 3-hour, 12-hour and 24-hour size. The longer the drying time, the shinier the gold will be when finished. It dries harder than water-based size. Remember that the drying times of size can vary according to atmospheric conditions.

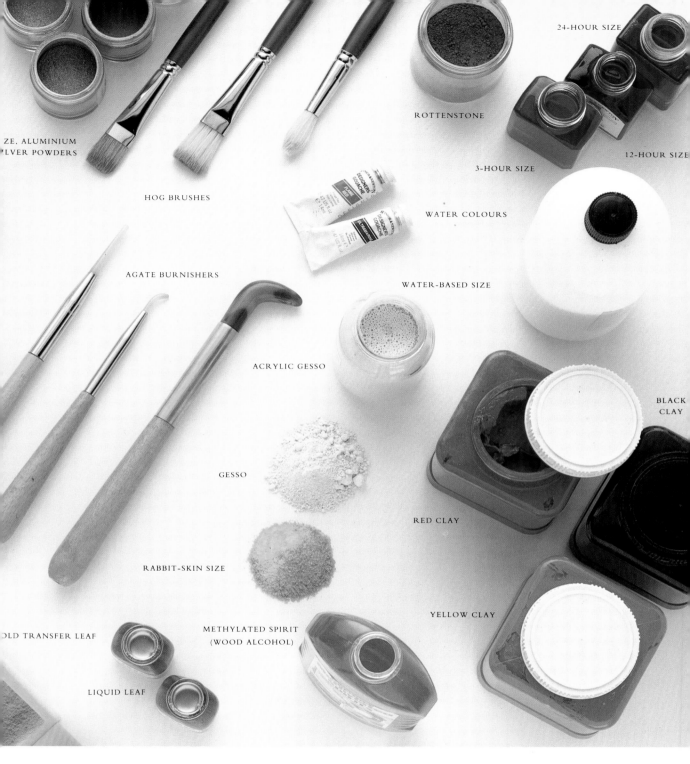

ZE, ALUMINIUM
ILVER POWDERS

HOG BRUSHES

AGATE BURNISHERS

ACRYLIC GESSO

GESSO

RABBIT-SKIN SIZE

OLD TRANSFER LEAF

LIQUID LEAF

METHYLATED SPIRIT
(WOOD ALCOHOL)

ROTTENSTONE

24-HOUR SIZE

3-HOUR SIZE

12-HOUR SIZE

WATER COLOURS

WATER-BASED SIZE

BLACK
CLAY

RED CLAY

YELLOW CLAY

TALC

This fine powder is applied to surfaces using a pounce bag made of very thin fabric and is patted on in an even layer. The talc is used to coat an area that is to be sized to ensure that the surface is clean and that only sized portions will take the gold or silver leaf.

GLOVES

Heavy-duty latex gloves are strongly recommended for stripping wood as protection against the chemicals present in the paint stripper. Lighter-weight gloves are useful to have for messy jobs, such as applying polish (shellac) which may stain your hands.

BASIC TECHNIQUES

THESE ARE THE BASIC techniques used in gilding and lacquering; individual projects give more detail where required. Before beginning a project, try to assemble all the equipment you will need in one place as this will allow for more efficient planning. Always work in a well-ventilated area and wear protective gloves and mask whenever necessary, particularly when stripping wood.

PREPARING RABBIT-SKIN SIZE FOR GESSO

This solution is used for all the different stages of water gilding. Prepare the size by mixing 55 g (2 oz) rabbit-skin size granules with 575 ml (1 pint) cold water in a metal bowl. Set the bowl in a pan of water, or bain-marie, and bring to the boil. Reduce the heat slightly and stir the solution while it simmers until the granules have completely melted and the size takes on a syrup-like consistency. This should take approximately 5-10 minutes. Leave to cool slightly. The size will become solid in a couple of hours. To keep for up to 2 days, leave in the refrigerator, covered with plastic film. The size will congeal in the cool temperature but to re-use reheat gently over a bain-marie.

PREPARING THE FIRST COAT OF GESSO

To prepare the first coat of gesso (also known as clearcole), add 1 part rabbit-skin size to 1 part cold water. Sieve in just enough gesso powder to colour the liquid. Stir well. When applied the gesso should appear translucent. Heat the liquid over a bain-marie until it is hot but not boiling. Apply to wood so that it penetrates the grain. Allow to dry overnight.

To prepare the first coat of gesso, sieve in just enough gesso powder to colour the rabbit-skin size

. . . .

APPLYING THE GESSO SOLUTION

Melt 2 parts rabbit-skin size to 1 part water, preferably in a large tin or metal container. Remove from the heat and sieve in the gesso powder until it rises above the surface of the mixture. Once this has been done, replace over the heat and stir gently with a hog brush to loosen the mixture and stir out any lumps.

Gesso solution should always be fairly warm when applied, but it should never be allowed to boil as this causes the water to evaporate and thickening to occur. If the gesso does become too thick, add about 50 ml (2 fl oz) water and stir gently until it becomes thin again.

Using a large hog brush, apply 6-12 coats, if possible all in the same day, making absolutely sure that each coat is completely dry before adding the next. You can tell when the gesso is dry when no grey areas remain and the gesso has turned white; this takes approximately 10 minutes per coat. Once finished, leave the piece to dry overnight.

To prepare the gesso solution, gently heat the rabbit-skin size and gesso powder mixture over a bain-marie until it is hot.

. . . .

Apply gesso solution to wood in an even coat so that it penetrates the grain.

. . . .

PUTTY

This is a type of filler, made from the same solution as gesso (i.e. 2 parts rabbit-skin size to 1 part water) but instead of gesso being applied to the solution, the solution is applied to the gesso. To do this, it is advisable to have a separate plate full of gesso powder. Make a small mound of gesso and then push a finger into the top to make a small hollow. Heat the solution in a bain-marie and pour a small amount into the hollow. Stir this with a spatula until the solution has picked up enough gesso powder to make a small ball of putty. Continue mixing the putty in your hand until it is smooth. Keep it in the palm of your hand to ensure that it stays warm and tacky.

When applying putty make sure that it is pressed onto the surface firmly so as to avoid any air getting in as this will make the putty crack on drying. Also make sure that you fill a hole by leaving a slightly raised surface to allow rubbing down flat afterwards.

PREPARING WOOD FOR PROJECTS

STRIPPING: if a piece of wooden furniture has been found with flaking or damaged paint, it needs to be treated before decorative work can start. When using stripping solutions it is important to work in a well-ventilated area; if possible wear a protective mask and gloves. Strip any old paint and polish using evenly applied paint stripper; avoid passing over any area twice. Allow the stripper to settle, following the manufacturer's instructions.

USING SOLVENTS FOR STRIPPING: sometimes pieces have been coated with waxes to protect the bare wood. These waxes will need to be removed using white (mineral) spirit and a coarse steel wool. Fine wet and dry sandpaper can be used to finish off.

FILLING: ready-made wood filler is easily available and useful for filling in rough grain, scratches and gashes. Alternatively you can make your own gesso putty filler (see Putty).

SANDING DOWN: any area that is to be decorated needs to be sanded down to create a smooth working surface. There are various grades and brands of sandpaper available. For sanding directly

on wood, use a low-grade paper, and finish off with a smoother paper, 240 or 320 grade. When sanding down gesso use wet and dry sandpaper to speed up the process. Do this by dipping the sandpaper into a bowl of lukewarm water and sanding normally. Pass over the wet surface with a dry rag to finish off and give an extra ivory-smooth quality to the piece.

APPLYING UNDERCOAT TO FURNITURE: before you undercoat a piece of furniture make sure the surface is clean and free of grease and wax. Wipe over the surface with white (mineral) spirit and a soft rag to remove any grime. If the piece of furniture needs filling it is a good idea to apply a coat of undercoat first to create a smooth surface. Allow the paint to dry and then fill with putty or filler wherever necessary. When the surface is smooth and clean, apply the second coat of undercoat. Use clean brushes. If the paint dries with a dusty surface, sand down with a fine-grade sandpaper before continuing.

T-CUT
This abrasive liquid is very good for smoothing varnishes. It helps reduce any dust which may have settled while the varnish is drying, and leaves a gloss surface with a pleasant hue.

Apply the T-cut with a soft rag or cotton wool (cotton balls), working slowly in sections. Wipe the surface with a clean soft rag and buff.

WATER GILDING
Water gilding is a process that involves the attaching of gold or silver leaf using gilding water as a fixing agent.

MAKING GILDING WATER: this is used to attach loose leaf in water gilding. To make gilding water, fill a container half-full of cold water. Slowly add methylated spirit (wood alcohol) until the water starts to change colour. Heat up some rabbit-skin size and add a teaspoon to the gilding water. Stir well until mixed.

APPLYING GOLD LEAF: paint a small amount of gilding water onto the surface where you wish to begin gilding. Gently place the leaf onto the dampened surface and press down lightly with cotton wool (cotton balls) every 5 minutes. Repeat this process until the whole surface is covered. Do not worry if there are small gaps as these can be patched afterwards using a sable brush and smaller pieces of leaf. When the area has been covered, leave the leaf to dry for about 1 hour.

CLAY SOLUTIONS
Clay solutions produce a smooth working surface for water gilding.

YELLOW CLAY: is prepared by melting 1 part prepared rabbit-skin size with 1 part water. Melt this in a metal container in a bain-marie so that some of the heat is retained during use. Once the size has melted, add just enough yellow clay to produce a mixture with the consistency of thick cream.

RED CLAY: This is prepared by melting 2 parts rabbit-skin size with 1 part water in a metal container in a bain-marie. As with yellow clay solution, add just enough red clay to produce a mixture with the consistency of thick cream. Mix well and apply with a sable brush.

OIL GILDING
Oil gilding involves the application of gold or silver leaf on top of a tacky size which holds the leaf in place before further decoration, burnishing or fixing takes place.

TALCING: when gilding only a small section of an item or applying a design to a piece of furniture, an application of talc through a pounce bag will help ensure that the surface is clean, dust and grease-free. The talc also means that only the areas that are sized will take gold or silver leaf so allowing for greater accuracy in its application.

Use a pounce bag to apply the talc, wiping over the area to be sized and spreading an even layer of powder. Remove any excess talc with a dusting brush or the palm of your hand. If the piece is newly painted or varnished, make sure that it is completely dry and that the talc is well rubbed in before applying size.

WATER-BASED SIZE: although this is a water-based size, the technique used is the same as that which incorporates oil-based size. The drying time of water-based size is 15-20 minutes at normal room temperature. The size is ready when it changes from being white to clear.

Water-based size can be mixed with water colour to form a base shade for transfer or loose leaf gold. To apply, brush on evenly and thinly (the size can be thinned with water); avoid laying on the size thickly as this will make the gold appear rough and bumpy. Brushes should be washed in warm, soapy water immediately after use.

OIL-BASED SIZE: this is available as 3-hour, 12-hour and 24-hour size. Drying times vary according to room temperature and atmospheric conditions although slight variations may occur depending on the brand of size used; it is best to always follow the manufacturer's instructions.

Oil-based size can be mixed with oil colours to form a tinted background for the gold or silver leaf. Beware, however, of adding too much colour as this affects the drying time. If adding oil colours, the size can be thinned slightly with white (mineral) spirit.

Apply the size thinly and evenly. After use, clean brushes in white (mineral) spirit and then rinse in warm, soapy water then clean water.

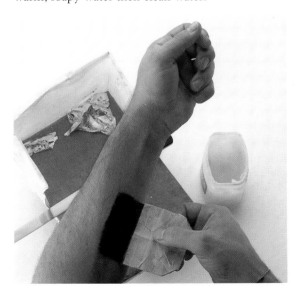

APPLYING LOOSE LEAF

Loose leaf can be applied using either water or oil gilding methods; a gilder's pad, knife and tip are extremely useful for the laying down of the leaves.

DROPPING LEAF ONTO THE GILDER'S PAD: any loose metal leaf can be handled on a gilder's pad, but particular care must be taken with gold leaf because it is so delicate. When using loose leaf make sure that there are no draughts of air that could blow the gold away. Check that your hands are dry and clean. Open the pages of the book over the pad and gently blow the leaf onto the surface of the pad. Do not blow too hard or this may split the leaf .

USING A GILDER'S KNIFE: loose leaves are often cut into smaller pieces before being applied to furniture. The gilder's knife must be quite free from grease; to clean it thoroughly and sharpen it at the same time, rub silicone carbide sandpaper 3-4 times along the knife blade. Do this when the knife is no longer cutting cleanly.

To cut loose leaf, pick up a leaf on the knife blade and put it in the centre of the gilder's pad. Blow gently until the leaf lies flat on the surface. Place the blade on the leaf and cut it by pulling the knife towards you once only.

USING A GILDER'S TIP: to facilitate picking up loose leaf, apply a small amount of petroleum jelly to your forearm. Brush the tip lightly over the petroleum jelly. This will help in picking up the loose leaf. Renew the petroleum jelly on the tip after every 5-6 applications of leaf.

Take the greased tip and place it flat on the piece of leaf. Place the tip, with the leaf on it, onto the hand which is holding the pad, putting the leaf between your index and middle fingers. The leaf should face outwards and downwards.

APPLYING TRANSFER LEAF

This is applied using either a stencil brush or your thumb (make sure your hands are clean and dry

. . . .

If you apply petroleum jelly to your forearm, the gilder's tip can be readily greased.

TOP: *Use a gilder's knife to cut loose leaf gold or silver by laying it on the gilder's pad and drawing the knife across the leaf once only.*

. . . .

ABOVE: *Lay loose leaf gold by first picking it up on the gilder's tip and then laying it down carefully in position.*

. . . .

first). Place the leaf over the size and press firmly. Hold the leaf in one hand and press with the other, taking care not to drag the metal.

FIXING GOLD OR SILVER LEAF AND LIQUID LEAF

Always apply fixing polish to gold and silver leaf which has been applied to any type of size. Do not varnish gold or silver powders or liquid leaf without first applying fixing polish or they will run and come away from the surface. It is also a good idea to apply polish before Indian ink decoration is applied. The individual projects describe how to mix the appropriate fixing polish for the various pieces of furniture and other items.

POLISH (SHELLAC)

If a gilded piece is to be varnished, waxed or have inked decoration applied, it must first receive a thorough application of polish (shellac) to prevent the leaf from wearing off. If you are polishing after gilding, make sure you use a tac-rag (a sticky cloth that will pick up dust and particles) or the palm of your hand to remove excess gold before polishing, otherwise the end result may be spoilt. Polish the decorated area by rubbing with a brush or a polishing rubber.

MAKING A POLISHING RUBBER

A polishing rubber is used to add extra shine to surfaces. To make a rubber, roll a small amount of synthetic wadding (batting) in your hand to form a pear shape. Wrap a piece of clean rag around this and leave it open at the top. Add transparent polish (shellac) to the wadding (batting) a few drops at a time until it is saturated. Wrap the rag tightly around the wadding (batting) to retain the pear shape. When the polish (shellac) starts to seep through, the rubber is ready for use and can be applied to the surface.

DISTRESSING GOLD

An aged and worn look can be achieved by gently rubbing a gilded surface with fine steel wool until the colour underneath is revealed. Distress the surface to a greater or lesser degree, depending on the finish desired. Fine sandpaper can also be used, and this is especially effective on liquid leaf as it dries to a hard finish.

White (mineral) spirit is also effective in producing a distressed appearance on gilding laid on size. Apply the spirit on a soft rag, rubbing in a circular motion. Work carefully and slowly as the leaf tends to come away suddenly. Fix the gilded surfaces after distressing is complete to retain the decorative effect.

JAPANNING

This process involves the application of layers of paint and varnish to achieve a smooth, glass-like finish. It is very important to prepare the surface properly before japanning as the final result is only as good as the preparation. The surface should be smooth and dust-free before painting begins. Each layer of paint should be sanded down lightly to remove any grit or dust which may have been picked up in the room or from a brush or dusty container. Use a tac-rag to remove the sanding dust. The layers of varnish in japanning can be made smooth by rubbing lightly with fine steel wool or silicone carbide sandpaper. A varnished japanned surface can be effectively smoothed down with an application of T-cut on cotton wool (cotton balls), and then buffed to a high shine with a soft rag.

VARNISHING

Use 2 brushes when varnishing, the first to apply the varnish, the other to brush it out so that it dries with a smooth surface. Varnishes can be used undiluted but it is advisable to thin them down with white (mineral) spirit for easier application. A better finish is produced from several layers of varnish rather than one thick coat.

To add colour to varnish, first spread the paint on the side of a small container using a small paintbrush, and then mix it into the varnish. This helps avoid uneven lumps of colour which may produce a patchy effect. This method of mixing colour can also be used with water-based size.

Be careful not to apply more varnish than is necessary, and always work in sections. The whole of large areas, such as table tops, should be varnished at once. Start varnishing at the top and work down. When using a coloured varnish, brush first horizontally then vertically to even out the colour. Apply varnish in well-ventilated room.

TRACING A DESIGN

Tracing is a very effective method of transferring a design from paper to a surface. Keep the design simple until you become confident in your decorative skills. There are several types of pattern books available everyday surroundings also provide inspiration in wallpaper and fabric designs, pieces of furniture or architectural details.

Having chosen a suitable design, decide whether it needs sizing up or down to fit the item to be decorated: patterns can be easily reduced or enlarged using a photocopier. Place a piece of tracing paper on top of the design and trace the design using a soft lead pencil. Turn the tracing over and position the design on the surface to be decorated. Fix it in place using strips of masking tape. Draw over the pattern using a hard lead pencil so that the soft lead lines on the reverse side are transferred to the surface.

An alternative to soft pencil lead is chalk pastel; draw the pattern onto the tracing paper using a pencil, and then rub chalk pastel over the reverse side Position the tracing paper on the surface as before, but without turning it over, and draw over the design again using a hard lead pencil.

GALLERY

The following pages show a collection of various pieces decorated by contemporary artists. Some of the objects have been constructed from scratch, others are adaptations of existing items, transformed by the application of an assortment of gold, silver and other metallic leaf. These leaves are often combined with applications of lacquer or with other, more unusual ornamentation. Each artist's style is individual, be it traditional, modern, nostalgic, influenced by far-off places and customs, or simply out of the ordinary.

These pieces are designed to encourage and inspire the new gilder or lacquer artist; the age-old techniques are not difficult to master and each style provides a stepping stone to other possibilities.

~

Lapis Blue and Gold Églomisé Pedestal
RUPERT BEVAN
This églomisé glass pedestal was inspired by the masculine styles of Tsarist Russia. The backs of the glass panels are painted a rich lapis blue to produce a particularly translucent effect.

Red Japanned Box with Gold Decoration

ROSARIA TITIAN

The simplicity of this red japanned box, decorated with oil gilding, epitomizes the originality and elegance of traditional Japanese screen painting.

. . . .

Silver Bust

GIUSEPPE MINETTI

This piece was produced using a mould taken from an antique carving and mounted on a frame. The bust is water gilded in silver and distressed to allow the splendid clay colours beneath to show through. The frame is painted in black with a speckling of silver varnished yellow to produce a rich gold effect.

. . . .

Gilded segments

NICHOLAS PHILLIPS
These ornate slices of
'cake' are decorated
using a variety of
painted colours and
surface features,
including a thick
gilded 'icing'.

. . . .

Heavenly Vacuum Cleaner

SHAUN CLARKSON
The application of gold
and mirrored mosaics has
transformed this
vacuum cleaner from
the mundane to the
magnificent.

. . . .

Silver Shell Table

ELIZABETH PORTER

This simple table displays *trompe-l'œil* shells. The table is decorated in loose leaf silver on size and painted in oil colours to produce an original and realistic decorative emblem.

. . . .

Ornate Seat

SARAH POTTS

This elegant upholstered seat is decorated in black with contrasting gilded lines that lead the eye around the curves of the furniture.

. . . .

Gilded Kettle

SHAUN CLARKSON

This kettle portrait is studded with glittering mirrored mosaic and, in contrast, is set within a traditional gilded frame.

. . . .

Coasters

RODRIGO AND
ROSARIA TITIAN

These coasters are ideal for practising various gilding and lacquering techniques; this selection is decorated in a combination of paint, gold and silver leaf and metallic powders to produce miniature works of art.

. . . .

TERRACOTTA POT

RODRIGO TITIAN

TRANSFER GOLD AND LOOSE LEAF SCHLAG (composition) leaf and bronze powders are often used to decorate wood, leather, metal and glass, but this project proves they can be applied to almost any material easily and effectively. This terracotta pot, which can be found in any garden centre or indeed in any home, is a good example of how to use leftover flakes of loose gold, schlag (composition) or aluminium leaf together with bronze powders to produce an original and attractive plant pot. If you want to use the pot outdoors, apply a heavy-duty exterior varnish after gilding.

~

1 Dust the terracotta pot and wipe it over with a soft rag soaked in a little methylated spirit (wood alcohol), just enough to remove any grease or dirt.

2 Using a small bristle brush, apply the first coat of black polish thinly and evenly, making sure there are no dribbles. You may want to wear household gloves when using black polish as it is very hard to remove from the skin. Allow 15-20 minutes for this coat to dry before applying a second coat in the same way. Black polish becomes tacky very quickly and is not like using oil-based paint. Make sure you work quickly and pass over an area only once unless it is completely dry.

3 Pour 60 ml (2½ fl oz) 15-minute water-based size into a jar. Using a large hog brush, mix some bronze powder into the white size, just enough to colour it. The bronze base coat will help to give the gold a deeper, more solid colour. You may need to add a small amount of water if it becomes too thick. Apply the size to the whole surface of the pot using the hog brush. Leave this for 10-15 minutes, or until it becomes tacky when touched.

4 Apply the gold, silver, aluminium and any other leaf in a haphazard manner. Add the gold transfer first, applying it in sections with a stencil brush, leaving some areas free to apply other golds or silver. If you have some loose leaf gold or silver, use a pad and tip to apply it.

5 Mix a fixing polish of 60 per cent methylated spirit (wood alcohol) to 40 per cent transparent polish (shellac) in a jar and apply a thin even coat to the pot using a polish brush. Make sure you cover the whole area thoroughly. The fixing polish remains shiny so that you can hold the pot against the light to make sure you have covered everywhere. A second coat can be applied for extra cover. Leave this to dry for about 20 minutes. Mix 30 ml (1 fl oz) gloss varnish with the same amount of white (mineral) spirit in a jar.

Using a small bristle brush, mix 2.5 cm (1 in) each of black and burnt umber oil colours in equal amounts into the gloss varnish to make a warm antique colour. Varnish the inside of the pot first using 2 medium bristle brushes, one to apply the varnish, the other as a dry brush for spreading out. Apply the varnish to the outside and again spread out with the dry brush. Make sure you brush vertically to finish off. Try to do this quickly, as the next stage has to be done when the varnish is still wet.

6 Dip a large hog brush into a small amount of white (mineral) spirit. Using your finger, flick the spirit onto the wet coloured varnish and wait for the colour to separate and produce a marbled effect. Use a dry soft clean rag to pat the surface of the pot in case the white (mineral) spirit starts to run. Do this in sections until the effect is achieved all over the pot. Leave to dry overnight. Apply a final coat of clear gloss varnish in the same way as the coloured varnish. Leave to dry.

PICTURE FRAME

RODRIGO TITIAN

A SIMPLE FLAT FRAME is used here. The application of the raised gesso motif is quite an old technique and the lines blend in well with the flowing brush strokes of the painting itself. The painting has been framed professionally and complements the soft yellow varnish used on the frame. The fact that silver leaf has been used below the yellow varnish gives the impression of the frame having been water gilded in gold leaf.

~

MATERIALS AND EQUIPMENT

- flat-sided picture frame
- putty or filler (optional)
- gesso • gesso brush
- tracing paper • soft lead pencil • small sable brush
- soft rags • yellow clay solution • large flat hog brush • black clay solution
- silicone carbide sandpaper
- dusting brush • gilding water • gilder's pad, knife and tip • petroleum jelly
- 2 books silver loose leaf
- cotton wool (cotton balls)
- small agate burnisher
- fine steel wool • methylated spirit (wood alcohol)
- transparent polish (shellac) • polishing rubber
- gloss varnish • white (mineral) spirit • small bristle brush • Indian yellow, crimson lake and burnt sienna oil colours
- badger brush
. . . . . .

1 If the frame has any cracks or chips that need filling repair them using putty or filler. Prepare the frame with a first coat of gesso and leave to dry for 24 hours. Then using a gesso brush, apply 4-6 coats of gesso in even generous strokes, leaving about half the amount for the next stages. Allow 15 minutes for each coat to dry before applying the next.

2 Choose a fairly simple design and transfer it to tracing paper. Transfer this to your frame with a soft lead pencil, making sure it is clear and sharp.

3 Heat the leftover gesso solution in a bain-marie until it becomes liquid. Using a small sable brush, apply the gesso to the lines of the design by dropping it on gently and gradually building it up until a raised motif is achieved. Allow to dry overnight. Rub down the gesso using a rag dipped into luke-warm water. Pass this over the frame in a circular motion until the gesso is ivory smooth. Allow to dry for 10 minutes.

4 Mix the yellow clay solution and heat it in a bain-marie. Using a large flat hog brush, apply this all over the surface of the frame as evenly as possible. Leave to dry for about 10 minutes. A second coat of yellow clay can be applied if a deeper colour is desired.

5 Mix and heat up the black clay solution in a bain-marie. When the mixture becomes liquid apply it to the raised motif only, using a small sable brush. Leave to dry for about 10 minutes.

6 Smooth down the clays using silicone carbide sandpaper until they are smooth to the touch. When you have done this, dust well with a dusting brush.

7 Mix the gilding water and add a pea-sized blob of yellow clay solution. Prepare your gilder's pad with a few sheets of silver leaf. Brush on the gilding water in small sections and, using the gilder's tip, lay on the silver cut to a rough size. After every 5 minutes of gilding, pat down the silver with cotton wool (cotton balls) to make sure there are no air bubbles. Allow between 1–2 hours to dry.

8 Using a small agate burnisher, burnish only the raised area.

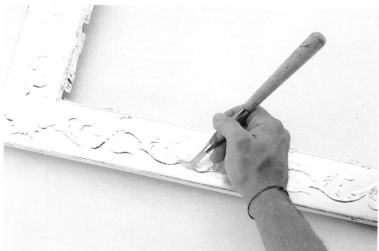

9 Distress the silver using steel wool. Do this until you can see the clay colours just coming through. Use a dusting brush to remove any steel wool fragments. Make some fixing polish by mixing 60 per cent methylated spirit (wood alcohol) with 40 per cent transparent polish (shellac) in a jar and apply a thin coat to fix the silver using a polishing rubber.

10 Mix a varnish of 50 per cent gloss varnish to 50 per cent white (mineral) spirit and, using a small bristle brush, add 2.5 cm (1 in) each of Indian yellow, crimson lake and burnt sienna oil colours to produce a yellow hue. Apply this to the frame using the same brush. Using a dry medium brush, spread the colour out evenly before it dries so as not to leave streaks or puddles.

11 Finally, use a badger brush to soften the colour and remove any varnish streaks, again making sure this is done before the varnish becomes touch-dry.

GILT KNIFE BOX

ROSARIA TITIAN

BOXES OF ALL SIZES AND SHAPES have for centuries been given as gifts or used as practical storage pieces. A large wooden box can be transformed into a beautiful heirloom, especially if it has a particularly decorative feature, such as a border in relief or pretty handles, which can be picked out in luminous gold or silver. Try experimenting with different combinations of lacquer and gilding to produce a variety of effects.

~

MATERIALS AND EQUIPMENT

- *wooden lidded box*
- *paint stripper (optional)*
- *gesso* • *soft rags*
- *silicone carbide sand-paper* • *yellow clay solution* • *large hog brush*
- *red clay solution* • *flat soft brush* • *fine steel wool*
- *dusting brush* • *gilding water* • *gilder's pad, knife and tip* • *petroleum jelly*
- *1 book loose leaf gold*
- *small sable brush*
- *cotton wool (cotton balls)*
- *agate burnisher* • *talc and pounce bag* • *3-hour size* • *yellow ochre oil colour* • *ruler (optional)*
- *1 book transfer gold leaf*
- *stencil brush* • *white (mineral) spirit* • *polishing rubber* • *transparent polish (shellac) (optional)* • *small bristle brush* • *gloss varnish*
- *clear wax* • *rottenstone*
. . . . . .

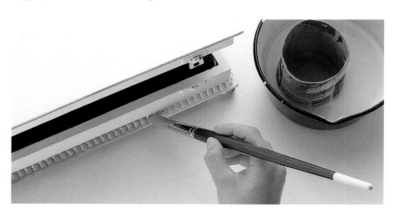

1 Remove old varnish from the box with paint stripper. Make sure the wood is dry and clean before you begin gessoing. Apply about 5-6 coats of gesso solution; this should be enough to cover the wood. Rub down with a damp rag and then with silicone carbide sandpaper.

2 Mix the yellow clay solution and heat slowly in a bain-marie. When the clay is liquid, and still warm, apply to the areas which will be water gilded, using a large hog brush. Cover the area well. Another coat may be added after about 10-15 minutes. Allow 15 minutes to dry.

3 Mix the red clay solution and heat slowly in a bain-marie. Apply the red clay over the yellow using a flat soft brush. Brush the red clay and leave this to dry for about 15 minutes.

4 Both the clays have to be smooth before the next stage. The red clay tends to dry slightly rough, so use steel wool rolled up in a small ball to rub the clays smooth. Use a dusting brush to take off the loose steel strands.

5 Prepare the gilder's pad with a few leaves of loose gold. Cut the gold leaf into 4 strips. Using a small sable brush, apply enough gilding water for 2 strips of gold to be laid at a time to a small section of the moulding.

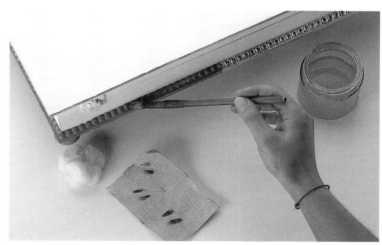

6 Lay on the gold with a gilder's tip. When 4 strips have been applied, pat down gently with a ball of cotton wool.

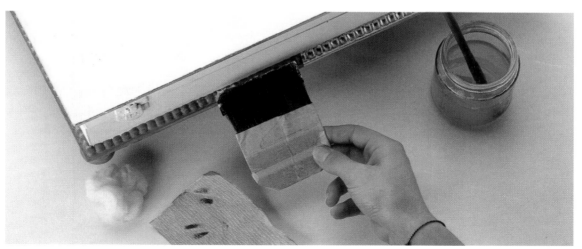

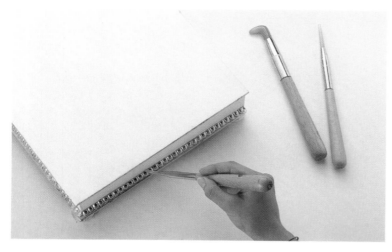

7 Wait about 1 hour before burnishing with an agate burnisher. The agate can be pressed quite hard on the gold. Rub it vigorously over the highlights until a high shine is achieved. If you find that the agate scratches the gold, leave it for another 15 minutes, as the clay below could still be wet from the gilding water.

8 Talc all the area to be oil gilded using a pounce bag. Pour 30 ml (1 fl oz) of 3-hour size into a tin and use a small sable brush to mix in about 2.5 cm (1 in) yellow ochre oil colour. A ruler can be used to draw a straight line border or else paint it freehand. If you make a mistake wait until the gold is applied before you tidy it up.

9 When the size has become tacky, about 2½-3 hours, place a sheet of transfer gold on the sized area, holding onto one corner of the leaf. Press firmly with a stencil brush or your thumb. When this is completed, pass your hand over the surface of the gold to remove any loose flakes. A little white (mineral) spirit on a rag can be used to tidy up wobbly lines.

10 Use a polishing rubber to fix the gold. Alternatively you can use a soft brush dipped in transparent polish (shellac). The gold will change in colour slightly when fixed and this should help you see where it has been polished. Make sure you are thorough, as the gold will come off when you varnish it if it has not been polished. Polish usually takes about 5–10 minutes to dry. Next paint on a coat of fairly thick gloss varnish, 80 per cent gloss varnish to 20 per cent white (mineral) spirit, using a small bristle brush. Leave to dry overnight.

11 To make the water gilding a warmer colour and to give it an antique feel, use clear wax and rottenstone. First, brush on the clear wax with a small bristle brush making sure it goes into the moulding.

12 Using a dry brush, pat the rottenstone. Use a substantial amount and when all the moulding has had the same treatment, wipe off the excess rottenstone lightly with a dry soft rag. The wax will hold some of the rottenstone in the mouldings to give it a dry dusty look.

ÉGLOMISÉ DESK

RODRIGO TITIAN

A PIECE OF BEAUTIFUL GLASS can transform an otherwise ordinary piece of furniture and protect its surface at the same time. The art of *verre églomisé*, the application of metal leaf and other decoration to glass, is a craft that dates back hundreds of years. It is used here with distressed silver-coloured leaf; the technique is simple yet produces an original and striking surface.

~

MATERIALS AND EQUIPMENT

- *old wooden desk with glass top (or glass cut to size)* • *paint stripper (optional)* • *filler (optional)* • *240 wet and dry sandpaper (optional)* • *wood glue (optional)* • *masking tape (optional)*

VERRE ÉGLOMISÉ:
- *soft rags* • *methylated spirit (wood alcohol)* • *gilder's pad, knife and tip* • *petroleum jelly* • *1 book loose leaf aluminium* • *gilding water* • *small bristle brush* • *ruler* • *dowel rod or pencil*

JAPANNING:
- *blue undercoat* • *medium bristle brush* • *silicone carbide sandpaper* • *dusting brush* • *blue eggshell (semi-gloss) paint* • *15-minute water-based size* • *silver powder* • *small sable brush* • *talc and pounce bag* • *pencil and ruler (optional)* • *1 book silver transfer leaf* • *stencil brush (optional)* • *fine steel wool (optional)* • *soft brush or polishing rubber* • *gloss varnish* • *white (mineral) spirit* • *Prussian blue and black oil colours* • *small bristle brush*

. . . . . .

1 Check the desk to make sure it is structurally sound. Strip any old paint or polish using paint stripper. Fill any dents or holes with filler and sand smooth. Any wobbly legs should be repaired with wood glue to make sure the loose joints are clean and dust-free. Any repairs can be secured with masking tape while drying.

2 Place the glass top on a flat surface. Clean the side to be gilded with a rag dampened with methylated spirit (wood alcohol). Prepare the gilding pad with a few leaves of aluminium. This leaf is heavier than gold leaf so make sure the gilder's tip is well coated with petroleum jelly. Pick up the whole leaf on the tip (do not cut it). Apply a good amount of gilding water with a small bristle brush, enough to lay about 2 leaves of aluminium.

3 Laying the leaf squarely takes time and practice, so do not worry if it folds as you can patch it up afterwards. Allow the leaf to just sink into the gilding water; do not pat it down. Leave overnight to dry thoroughly.

4 Use your fingers in a circular motion to distress the aluminium. It is not necessary to press very hard, and the loose aluminium should come away with ease.

5 Place a ruler 2.5 cm (1 in) away from the edge of the glass, making sure it is the same distance from top to bottom. Use a sharpened dowel rod or a pencil to scratch a line along the edge of the ruler. Keeping the ruler steady, use a damp rag to remove the silver edge. Do this all the way around the edge of the glass.

6 Paint the desk with the first
coat of blue undercoat using
a medium bristle brush. Start
from the top and work your way
down. Leave to dry overnight.
Rub down lightly with a sheet of
silicone carbide sandpaper. Dust
with a dusting brush before
applying the second coat of
undercoat. Leave to dry and rub
down again before applying the
blue eggshell (semi-gloss). Paint
this on by first brushing
vertically, spreading the paint
evenly, then horizontally using
much lighter strokes. This
prevents the paint from
becoming streaky. Leave to dry
in a well-ventilated room.

7 Pour 50 ml (2 fl oz)
15-minute water-based size
into a container. Add 2 teaspoons
of silver powder and mix well
with a small sable brush. Using a
pounce bag, talc the surface of
the desk to remove any tacky
areas. Decorate the legs, drawers
and top edge with straight border
lines. The silver powder
colouring the size will help you
see where you have painted and
it will also give the silver a more
solid look. You can try painting
lines freehand but this takes a
steady hand and practice; if you
find it easier draw out the lines
with a pencil and ruler.

8 Use a stencil brush or your
thumb to press the transfer
silver leaf onto the size.

9 Roll a small amount of fine steel wool into a ball. Rub the silver lightly until you achieve a distressed look. You can omit this stage if a cleaner, brighter look is preferred. Fix the silver with a soft brush or a polishing rubber.

10 Mix 100 ml (4 fl oz) gloss varnish with 100 ml (4 fl oz) white (mineral) spirit in a container. Squeeze 2.5 cm (1 in) each of Prussian blue and black oil colours onto a small bristle brush. Mix the colours on the side of the container and then into the varnish. Apply the varnish in sections starting from the top and working your way down. Paint on just enough to cover the area you are working on, as too much will cause dribbles and puddles. Use a dry bristle brush to brush out the varnish evenly. Leave this overnight in a well-ventilated dust-free room. Apply a final coat of varnish, made up of 60 per cent gloss varnish and 40 per cent white (mineral) spirit. When dry, place the glass silver side down.

STANDARD LAMP

GIUSEPPE MINETTI

THIS STANDARD LAMP was found in an attic, covered in pink paint. It had to be stripped down to the wood, and re-wired with up-to-date wiring. A clever playing-card theme has been used to decorate it. The green base colour was chosen with the green felt of a card table in mind, and silver and lemon metallic powders were mixed with red and black oil colours so that the shapes and colours matched a pack of cards.

~

MATERIALS AND EQUIPMENT

• *1 standard lamp* • *paint stripper (optional)* • *fine steel wool* • *methylated spirit (wood alcohol)* • *filler (optional)* • *green undercoat paint* • *large bristle brush* • *240 wet and dry sand-paper (optional)* • *600 wet and dry sandpaper* • *dusting brush* • *medium bristle brush* • *green eggshell (semi-gloss) paint* • *gloss varnish* • *white (mineral) spirit* • *black and bright red oil colours* • *badger brush* • *tracing paper* • *hard lead pencil* • *white chalk pastel* • *masking tape* • *lemon powder* • *small bristle brush* • *small sable brush* • *silver powder* • *soft rags* · · · · · ·

1 If necessary, strip the wood of paint and polish using paint stripper, steel wool and methylated spirit (wood alcohol). Make sure the wood is clean and dry before applying the first coat of paint. Check to see if the lamp has any holes which need filling; if so use filler for this.

2 Paint on the first coat of green undercoat using a large bristle brush, making sure this covers the wood evenly. Allow to dry overnight. Fill any holes as necessary and leave the filler for about 1 hour so it is completely dry, and then sand down with 240 wet and dry sandpaper. Sand down the rest of the painted surface with 600 wet and dry sandpaper until it is smooth to the touch. Use a dusting brush to remove the dust. Paint on the second coat of green undercoat and leave to dry. Once dry, sand down lightly with 600 wet and dry sandpaper and dust again.

3 Using a medium bristle brush, apply a coat of green eggshell (semi-gloss) paint, brushing it on in sections, brushing first horizontally then vertically. Try not to brush the eggshell (semi-gloss) out too much as it will dry with visible brush marks. It tends to dry smoother than it looks so do not fuss too much with it. Leave to dry for 12 hours, then sand down lightly with 600 wet and dry sandpaper. Dust again with the dusting brush.

4 Mix 60 ml (2½ fl oz) gloss varnish with 60 ml (2½ fl oz) white (mineral) spirit. Reserve half of this in another container. Using a medium bristle brush, mix 1.5 cm (½ in) black oil colour into one portion of the varnish. Apply a small amount of coloured varnish to the lamp in sections, making sure you work quickly and evenly, brushing both horizontally and vertically.

5 Use a dry badger brush to soften the colour so that the brush marks disappear – try to stipple the varnish with the badger brush. Also brush it vertically and horizontally. The varnish must not become dry while you are doing this as it will leave marks, so work quickly and in small sections. Allow to dry overnight in a dust-free well-ventilated room.

6 Choose your design and transfer it to some tracing paper using a sharp hard lead pencil. Use a white chalk pastel to draw the shape of the design on the reverse of the tracing paper. It does not matter if it is not neat as long as all of the design is covered in chalk pastel. Turn over the tracing paper and place it on the lamp where you want the design. Hold it steady with your hand or use strips of masking tape to keep it still while you trace the design. Remove the tracing paper and you should have a clear, sharp image transferred onto the lamp.

7 Place half of the remaining varnish in a container. Add 2 teaspoons of lemon powder to the varnish and mix in well with a small bristle brush. Pick out the mouldings with a small sable brush, using just the varnish and lemon powder. Leave to dry overnight.

8 Add 1.5 cm (½ in) bright red oil colour to the remaining lemon and varnish mixture and mix well. Paint the heart and diamond design in this colour using a small sable brush.

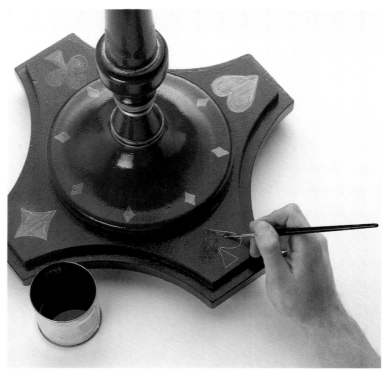

9 Add 2 teaspoons of silver powder to the remaining varnish and mix this with 1.5 cm (½ in) black oil colour. Paint the clubs and spades using a small sable brush. Make sure you clean the brush after using the lemon powder by wiping it in a rag soaked in white (mineral) spirit.

10 Pour 60 ml (2½ fl oz) gloss varnish into a clean container and mix in 60 ml (2½ fl oz) white (mineral) spirit. You can use clear varnish alone or add a little black to the varnish to make the effect darker. Use a small bristle brush to apply the varnish and a medium bristle brush to brush it out. Apply the varnish in sections and check after each section for dribbles, using the dry brush to soften the varnish lines.

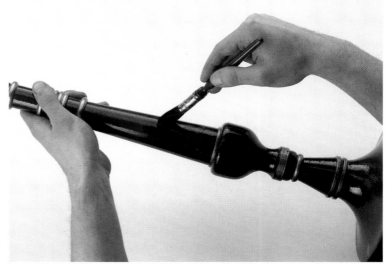

OVAL MIRROR FRAME

DARIO ARNESE

HOW MANY TIMES have you stopped to look at a piece of furniture in your home and contemplated moving it or throwing it out altogether? This mirror frame will encourage anyone to take the time to look at a shape and consider the possibilities of transforming a rather mundane object into a striking centrepiece. The combination of water gilding and lacquer adds elegance to this frame and picks out the delicate relief work.

~

MATERIALS AND EQUIPMENT

- *oval frame* • *putty or filler (optional)* • *240 wet and dry sandpaper* • *gesso*
- *medium bristle brush*
- *silicone carbide sandpaper*
- *yellow clay solution* • *red clay solution* • *medium synthetic brush* • *dusting brush* • *gilding water*
- *rabbit skin size*
- *2 books loose leaf gold*
- *gilder's pad, knife and tip*
- *petroleum jelly*
- *cotton wool (cotton balls)*
- *agate burnisher* • *fine steel wool* • *large synthetic brush* • *black eggshell (semi-gloss) paint* • *soft rags*
- *gloss varnish* • *white (mineral) spirit* • *small bristle brush* • *burnt umber oil colour* • *clear wax*

. . . . . .

1 Check to see that the frame does not need any attention before starting. If it needs filling, apply putty or filler and allow to dry for 30 minutes. Smooth down with 240 wet and dry sandpaper.

2 Prepare the first coat of gesso. Leave it in a saucepan to keep it hot. Using a medium bristle brush, apply to the frame and allow to dry overnight. Prepare the gesso and keep warm in a saucepan. Using a medium bristle brush, apply 6 coats of gesso, allowing each coat to dry before applying the next. Allow the final coat to dry for at least 2 hours, then rub down smooth using first 240 wet and dry sandpaper, then silicone carbide to finish off. Mix the yellow clay solution in a tin and heat up in a saucepan over direct heat. Brush on 2 coats of yellow clay using a medium bristle brush. Cover the gesso completely, leaving no trace of it showing through.

3 Heat the red clay solution and brush on 2 coats using a medium synthetic brush. Apply this to the highlights of the frame only, trying not to get the clay in the crevices. Allow to dry for 15–20 minutes.

4 Using silicone carbide sandpaper, sand down the red and yellow clays until they are smooth to the touch. Remove the dust with a dusting brush.

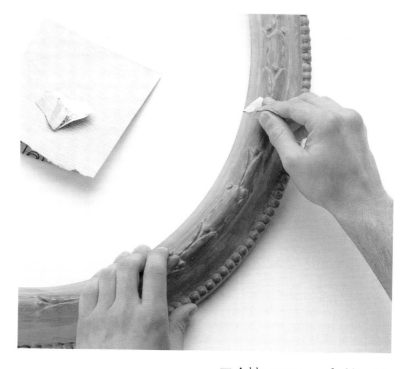

5 Add a teaspoon of rabbit-skin size to the gilding water. Drop some leaves of gold onto the gilder's pad and blow out a sheet so that it lies flat. Cut the leaf into 3 parts and pick up a piece with the gilder's tip. Using a medium soft synthetic brush, brush the gilding water onto the area to be gilded, then apply the gold leaf to the frame.

6 Once you have applied about 6 pieces of gold leaf (2 sheets), pat down the gold with rolled up pieces of cotton wool (cotton balls) to get rid of any air bubbles. Make sure the cotton is not wet from the patting down or it may remove the freshly applied gold.

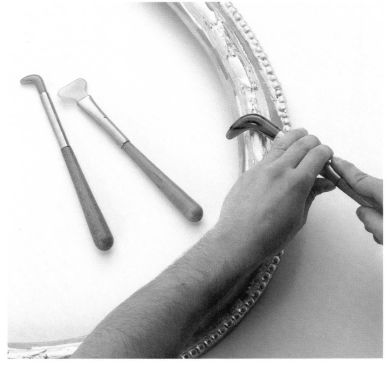

7 Once you have finished gilding the whole frame, wait for the gold to dry, about 1 hour (depending on weather conditions), then burnish with an agate burnisher passing it over the gold a number of times until the gold starts to shine. Do not press too hard as this will only weaken the gesso below.

8 If you want to make the gold look older, distress it by passing over it a few times with steel wool. Make sure you do not do this in even strokes because it looks false, so rub the steel wool in circular motions as well as vertically.

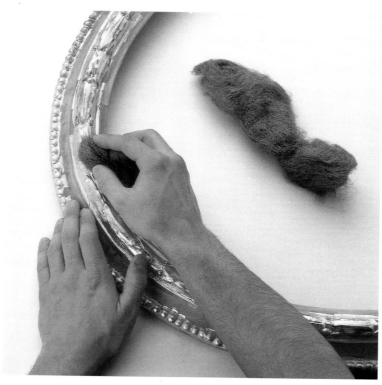

9 With a large soft synthetic brush apply a base coat of black eggshell (semi-gloss) paint. Leave to dry overnight. Apply a second coat of eggshell, making sure no dribbles occur and that any smudges that may have gone into the gold are wiped off with a rag.

10 Mix 30 ml (1 fl oz) gloss varnish with 30 ml (1 fl oz) white (mineral) spirit in a container. Use a small bristle brush to mix 1.5 cm (½ in) burnt umber oil colour into the varnish. Brush onto the black eggshell (semi-gloss) using one bristle brush to brush on and another dry one to brush out. Use a dry rag to wipe off any varnish which may be on the gold. Leave to dry overnight. Wax the whole of the frame using a small bristle brush to apply the wax and a soft clean rag to buff it up. Mount a mirror in the frame and hang.

STARS AND MOON
BOWL

GIUSEPPE MINETTI

THE ANCIENT ART of applying dusted gold to lacquer and producing a design from layers of powders can be successfully adapted to decorate modern household ware. The quality of the original Japanese technique known as *makie* is very difficult to match as it required hours of careful specialist work by the most highly skilled of craftsmen. However, a most effective substitute can be easily created at very little expense and with only a small amount of practice.

~

MATERIALS AND EQUIPMENT

• *large metal bowl* • *soft rags* • *methylated spirit (wood alcohol)* • *red oxide metal primer* • *small bristle brush* • *white (mineral) spirit* • *black eggshell (semi-gloss) paint* • *15-minute water-based size* • *soft synthetic brush* • *gold powder* • *large sable brush* • *talc and pounce bag* • *tracing paper* • *soft lead pencil* • *hard lead pencil* • *silver powder* • *transparent polish (shellac)* • *newspaper* • *small sable brush* • *classic gold liquid leaf* • *gloss varnish*

. . . . . .

1 Clean the bowl with a rag and methylated spirit (wood alcohol) to remove any grease or dirt.

2 Apply a coat of red oxide metal primer using a small bristle brush. If the primer seems too thick, thin it down with a few drops of white (mineral) spirit. Try to apply the primer as smoothly and evenly as possible, working from the centre of the bowl to the edge. Wait for this to be touch-dry before painting the outside of the bowl. This makes it easier to handle. Leave to dry. Metal primers vary in drying time so read the manufacturer's instructions before starting the next stage.

3 Paint on black eggshell (semi-gloss) paint in the same way as the metal primer. Spread the paint evenly and try to use the tip of the brush in the final strokes to soften the brush marks. Leave to dry and apply a second coat of eggshell in the same way.

4 Turn the bowl upside-down and paint 15-minute water-based size all over the outside of the bowl with a soft synthetic brush. When the size has become transparent after about 15–20 minutes, lightly brush on gold powder using a large sable brush and dust with talc.

5 Transfer your design to the tracing paper with a soft lead pencil. Turn the tracing paper over and place on the talced bowl. Keeping the paper flat, transfer the design by firmly drawing on the pencilled area with a hard pencil. Trace the moon and star shapes at random all over the inside of the bowl.

6 Paint the traced design with 15-minute water-based size using a soft synthetic brush.

7 Use a dry sable brush to brush the gold powder onto the star shapes and silver powder onto the moon shapes.

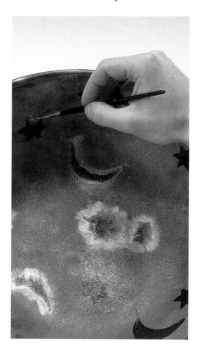

8 When all the sized areas are covered with powder, use a soft synthetic brush to take off any loose powder.

9 Fix all the layers of gold and silver powder by carefully brushing on fixing polish made up of 80 per cent transparent polish (shellac) and 20 per cent methylated spirit (wood alcohol). Use a soft synthetic brush. Do not load your brush with too much polish as this will collect and dry in ridges – dab the wet brush onto some clean newspaper before applying it to the bowl. Do not brush the same area more than a couple of times. Cover it thoroughly and thinly. If you have missed any areas wait for

the first coat to dry well, about 20 minutes, before applying a second coat.

Paint the outlines of the stars and moons to emphasize the shapes using a small sable brush and classic gold leaf (liquid leaf comes in other colours if preferred). Shake the bottle of liquid leaf well as the colour tends to sink to the bottom. This can be thinned down with a few drops of white (mineral) spirit. This also helps the liquid leaf to stay runny for a longer period of time. Leave to dry for about 20

minutes. Use a clean small sable brush to fix the liquid leaf with fixing polish as before. Make sure this is covered well otherwise applying the varnish will make it run. Give it 2 coats of polish if you want to be sure. Leave for 10 minutes. Pour 60 ml (2½ fl oz) gloss varnish into a container. Add to this 2 teaspoons of white (mineral) spirit and mix well. Brush on with a small bristle brush and brush out evenly and thoroughly with a dry brush.

SUNBURST TABLE

ELIZABETH PORTER

THIS SMALL TABLE has been transformed into an oil painting on legs. This means of decorating objects can be easily adapted for any piece from a chair to a mirror to a glass vase, with equally striking results. The table is a perfect example of how old techniques adapt wonderfully to modern designs. Here ink and shadowing play an important part in the final result which is one of fun and charm.

~

1 Find a plain wooden table and fill and sand as necessary.

2 Apply a coat of yellow ochre undercoat using a medium bristle brush. Allow to dry overnight. This first coat of paint will raise the grain and make it feel furry. Using 600 wet and dry sandpaper, rub down the surface until it becomes smooth. Wipe down the surface with a dry rag, apply a second coat of undercoat and leave it to dry.

MATERIALS AND EQUIPMENT

• *wooden table* • *filler (optional)* • *600 wet and dry sandpaper* • *yellow ochre undercoat* • *medium bristle brushes* • *soft rags* • *small bristle brush* • *gloss varnish* • *crimson lake, Indian yellow, burnt sienna and black oil colours* • *medium sable brush* • *badger brush* • *talc and pounce bag* • *tracing paper* • *hard lead pencil* • *white chalk pastel* • *small sable brush* • *3-hour size* • *gilder's pad, knife and tip* • *petroleum jelly* • *1 book loose leaf white gold* • *1 book loose leaf gold* • *methylated spirit (wood alcohol)* • *transparent polish (shellac)* • *polishing rubber* • *gloss varnish* • *white (mineral) spirit* • *black Indian ink* • • • • • •

3 Using a small bristle brush, mix 60 ml (2½ fl oz) gloss varnish with equal amounts of crimson lake, Indian yellow and burnt sienna oil colours. Mix well. Using a clean medium bristle brush paint on the varnish evenly, starting on the top of the table. Next brush horizontally then vertically with a dry bristle brush.

4 Prepare a palette with a little black oil colour on one side. Mix the coloured varnish with the black oil colour in the plate with a medium sable brush. Blob the black colour onto the wet varnish. This has to be done quickly before the varnish becomes too tacky.

5 While the layers of varnish are still wet, soften lightly with a badger brush. Paint the rest of the table in the same way. Leave to dry overnight in a well-ventilated dust-free room.

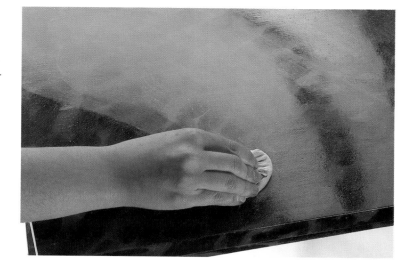

6 Use a pounce bag to talc over the surface to be decorated. Pass your hand over the talc to remove any excess.

7 Transfer your design clearly onto a sheet of tracing paper. On the reverse side, draw out the design using a white chalk pastel. This will show up better on a dark surface. Place the tracing paper – chalky side face down – onto the talc-covered surface. Using a sharp, hard lead pencil draw the sunburst and clouds onto the table, making sure that the design is central and straight.

8 Use a small sable brush to cover the clouds in 3-hour size. Ensure the chalk pastel is not rubbed off while applying the size.

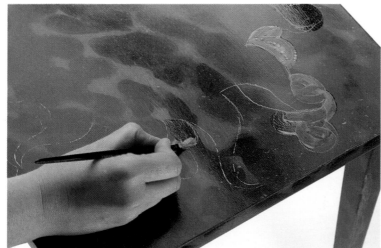

9 When the size is tacky, approximately 2½-3 hours, lay on the white gold. Use a gilder's tip to apply the leaf. Use your fingers to rub in the white gold to ensure it has stuck down on all the sized areas and to remove the loose excess flakes.

10 Paint the sunburst pattern with 3-hour size. When the size is tacky apply the gold leaf in the same way as the white gold. When all the sized areas are gilded, wipe over with a dry soft rag or the palm of your hand. Ensure there are no loose bits of gold before you apply fixing polish of 60 per cent methylated spirit (wood alcohol) with 40 per cent transparent polish (shellac) – using a polishing rubber.

11 Trace the face of the sunburst onto the gold in the same way as before. Use a small sable brush with a good point to draw in the face and to outline the sunburst design in black Indian ink. If you make a mistake wipe it off with a damp rag. Do this immediately as the ink dries quite quickly.

12 Mix 60 ml (2½ fl oz) gloss varnish with 30 ml (1 fl oz) white (mineral) spirit. Use a little of this varnish to mix burnt sienna oil colour on a palette. Mix this into a thin wash of colour. Paint on the shadows using a small sable brush and leave to dry overnight. Apply a coat of the ready-mixed varnish to the top first, then work your way down using one small bristle brush to apply the varnish and another dry bristle brush to brush it out evenly.

SILVER BOX

ELIZABETH PORTER

THIS SIMPLE WOODEN BOX was rescued from the scrap pile and transformed into a shimmering table ornament. Faux mother-of-pearl is created by combining silver leaf and delicate applications of oil colours. By layering the tones and shades in various depths of intensity, the translucent quality of pearl shell is produced momentarily with the illusion of *trompe-l'œil.*

~

MATERIALS AND EQUIPMENT

- *wooden pencil box*
- *600 wet and dry sandpaper* • *soft rags*
- *black (shellac) polish*
- *small bristle brush*
- *3-hour gold size* • *silver transfer leaf* • *stencil brush*
- *transparent polish (shellac)* • *methylated spirit (wood alcohol)* • *soft synthetic brush or polish brush* • *gloss varnish*
- *white (mineral) spirit*
- *crimson lake, ultramarine, black and raw umber oil colours* • *small sable brush* • *badger brush*
- *T-cut*

. . . . . .

1 Give the box a light rub using 600 wet and dry sandpaper. Dust with a clean rag.

2 Apply a coat of black (shellac) polish, using a small bristle brush. One coat should be enough but if it has not covered well wait 10 minutes before applying a second coat. Rub the surface down very lightly with sandpaper.

3 Paint 3-hour gold size all over the box using a small bristle brush. Check to make sure the size has covered the whole area. Leave the box for 3 hours.

4 Place the silver leaf flat onto the sized box. Press a stencil brush firmly on the silver leaf brushing in one direction away from the hand that is holding the edge of the backing sheet. Cover the whole of the outside of the box in the same way. Use the palm of your hand or a clean, soft rag to smooth down the flaky silver. Any touching up of missed areas should be done now.

5 Mix 60 ml (2½ fl oz) transparent polish (shellac) with 30 ml (1 fl oz) methylated spirit (wood alcohol). Mix together well. Use a soft synthetic brush or a polish brush to apply the polish. Brush on thoroughly and evenly.

6 Mix together 60 ml (2½ fl oz) gloss varnish with 30 ml (1 fl oz) white (mineral) spirit. Have a plate ready with crimson lake, ultramarine, black and raw umber oil colours. Put 1.5 cm (½ in) or less on the plate and use a small sable brush to mix the colours with a little of the gloss varnish solution. Make each colour into a thin wash, keeping the shades separate. Dot on the colours in layers, the first being the weakest in colour. Cover the whole surface in small sections so that you work on wet varnish for all the layers. Paint the second layer using stronger colours but only covering parts of the surface so the thinner wash underneath is still visible.

7 Soften the varnish while it is still wet by lightly brushing a badger brush over the surface. Cover the whole box in the same way; 2-3 layers should be enough. Leave to dry overnight.

8 Pour 60 ml (2½ fl oz) gloss varnish into a container and add 1.5 cm (½ in) ultramarine and the same amount of raw umber oil colour. Mix well with a small bristle brush. Paint on the varnish evenly and quite thickly for a glass-like finish. Before you leave this to dry, make sure there are no dribbles. If there are, use a dry bristle brush to spread them out. Allow to dry overnight. T-cut the varnish, then paint on a final coat of clear gloss varnish.

LACQUERED TROLLEY

ROSARIA TITIAN

THE USE OF RAISED MOTIFS on lacquer dates back eight hundred years. This trolley is decorated using a simplified form of the Japanese technique *taki-maki* which consists of building up layers of gesso to produce a low relief. The floral motifs used here are fairly simple; traditional patterns also include birds and figures decorated in gold, silver and bronze. Your design can be simplified or made more complex depending on your time and patience.

~

MATERIALS AND EQUIPMENT

- *trolley* • *coarse steel wool*
- *methylated spirit (wood alcohol)* • *paint stripper (optional)* • *gesso*
- *medium bristle brush*
- *240 wet and dry sandpaper* • *hard lead pencil* • *soft lead pencil*
- *tracing paper* • *small sable brush* • *soft rags*
- *15-minute water-based size* • *small bristle brush*
- *Venetian red water colour or gouache* • *talc and pounce bag* • *dusting brush*
- *ruler (optional)* • *1 book lemon gold transfer leaf*
- *stencil brush (optional)*
- *gloss varnish* • *white (mineral) spirit* • *silver powder* • *black Indian ink*
- *raw umber, Indian yellow and burnt sienna and black oil colours* • *large bristle brush*

. . . . . .

1 Check that the structure of the piece is stable, and see whether it needs stripping before being gessoed. There are firms that will strip furniture for you and this is a very good option because it is not expensive and the final result is usually very good. Remember, though, that most wood-stripping places dip the furniture into caustic soda which has to be neutralized with vinegar before applying gesso.

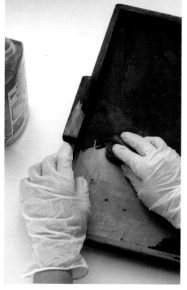

2 If you decide to strip the piece yourself make sure you do it outside, although smaller pieces, such as boxes, can be stripped in a cool well-ventilated room. Wear protective gloves. If the paint or polish is only a very thin coat, remove this by using coarse steel wool and methylated spirit (wood alcohol). Allow the spirit (alcohol) to sink into the paint. Press the steel wool hard onto the surface to remove the layers. For thicker coats of paint you may need a paint stripper.

3 Prepare the gesso in a bain-marie. Before you start gessoing make sure the surface is dry and clean. Apply 6 coats of gesso using a medium bristle brush. When dry, rub down with 240 wet and dry sandpaper until an ivory-like finish is achieved. Trace the design for the trays directly onto the gesso. Check that it is central and straight.

4 Heat the remaining gesso until it becomes liquid. Using a small sable brush, drop the gesso into some of the leaf and flower design. Build up the gesso while it is still wet. Concentrate on one leaf or flower at a time until it is built up before moving on to the next. The gesso will dry flatter so make sure you drop on enough to achieve a raised effect. This takes some time so keep the tin of gesso in a pan with hot water and keep re-heating it when it cools down. When finished, leave to dry overnight. When the gesso is dry use a damp rag to smooth down; this will also help to fill any air bubbles.

5 Pour 30 ml (1 fl oz) 15-minute water-based size into a container. Use a small bristle brush to mix in 1.5 cm (½ in) of Venetian red water colour. Colouring the size helps to make it visible when applied and gives the gold a deep, warm look. Talc the whole surface, including the trays, using a pounce bag. Use a dusting brush to remove the excess paint on the lines of the trolley itself. Draw the straight lines freehand, or use a pencil and ruler if you prefer, to decorate the edges and legs of the trolley.

6 After 15-20 minutes press the lemon gold transfer onto these lines using a stencil brush or your thumb.

7 Apply more size to the raised motif on the base of the trays and to the rest of the design, leaving some of the leaves white. Use a smaller sable brush to paint the finer details. If you make a mistake at this stage wait until the lemon gold is applied before you correct it. You can then remove any errors with a damp rag.

9 Pour 30 ml (1 fl oz) gloss varnish and the same amount of white (mineral) spirit into a small dish and add enough silver powder to colour the varnish. Mix together. Test a small area on the tray to make sure it covers well. Paint the remaining pencilled decoration in silver using a small sable brush. Allow to dry overnight.

8 Lay a sheet of lemon gold over the size, again using either a stencil brush or your thumb to press it into place.

The gold should be the only part of the sheet in contact with the size but take care or the backing paper will stick to the size.

10 Fix the lemon gold with polish. It is a good idea to fix the gold before any ink is applied as the ink tends to break up when applied directly onto the gold; any mistakes can be removed without taking off the gold. Use a fine sable brush with a good point to paint on the veins of the leaves and decorate the flowers using black Indian ink. Have a small container of water to clean the ink brush every now and then. Dry the brush with a rag before continuing your inking.

11 Distress the ink and lemon gold with a little white (mineral) spirit on a rag. Rub the gold gently until the red colour comes through.

13 Wipe over the surface with a rag to remove any dust. Use the rest of the varnish from the day before to mix the final colour. Squeeze 1.5 cm (½ in) each of burnt sienna, raw umber, Indian yellow, and 6 mm (¼ in) of black oil colour onto a small bristle brush, mix with the varnish and paint on evenly.

12 Pour 100 ml (4 fl oz) gloss varnish into a container, add the same amount of white (mineral) spirit and mix well. Pour a little of this into a jar, covering the rest of the varnish with a lid or plastic film. Use the varnish to mix the colour for the shadows. Squeeze 1.5 cm (½ in) of raw umber and Indian yellow onto a plate or palette.

Mix a bit of the 2 colours in equal amounts on the plate with a small sable brush. Mix these colours into a thin wash; if the colour looks too strong add more varnish. Paint just fewer than half the leaves in this colour and part of the flowers to achieve a two-dimensional effect. Leave to dry overnight.

14 Using a large dry bristle brush, spread the varnish evenly by brushing horizontally and then vertically to soften the colour. Varnish the trolley in sections to avoid the varnish sticking while you are still brushing out. Leave to dry overnight in a well-ventilated dust-free room.

JAPANESE-STYLE SCREEN

ROSARIA TITIAN

SCREENS ARE MOVING BACK into our homes, as both decorative furnishings and draught excluders. This screen can even be hung flat against a wall to provide a beautiful decorative expanse. The ornate effects are derived from the ancient Japanese art of gilding a surface and then painting a design with oil colours directly onto the gold. The end result is one of brilliance and simplicity combined.

~

MATERIALS AND EQUIPMENT

• *leather, wood or canvas screen* • *dark red eggshell (semi-gloss) paint* • *large bristle brush* • *soft rags* • *12-hour size* • *200 leaves schlag (composition) leaf* • *gilder's pad, knife and tip* • *petroleum jelly* • *small soft brush* • *newspaper* • *white (mineral) spirit* • *transparent polish (shellac)* • *methylated spirit (wood alcohol)* • *polish brush* • *tracing paper* • *hard lead pencil* • *red chalk pastel* • *burnt sienna, black, burnt umber and Indian yellow oil colours* • *medium bristle brush* • *gloss varnish* • *small sable brush* • *badger brush* • • • • • •

2 Dust the screen with a soft rag. Apply 12-hour size using a large bristle brush. Evenly cover the whole screen including the edges. Leave the size for approximately 12 hours to become tacky.

1 Check the surface of the screen for holes or dents and fill or repair as necessary before beginning to decorate. Apply 2 coats of dark red eggshell (semi-gloss) paint using a large bristle brush. Leave to dry thoroughly.

3 Place 2-3 leaves of schlag (composition) leaf onto a gilding pad. Use the gilder's tip to lay the leaf flat. This leaf is heavier than loose leaf gold so have the gilder's tip well covered in petroleum jelly to make it easier to pick up the leaf. Pick up the whole leaf and carefully lay it on the size, starting from the top left-hand corner and working down. Cover one panel at a time and try to lay the leaf as squarely as possible.

4 Before brushing off any loose flakes of leaf with a small soft brush, put down a layer of newspaper beneath the screen so that the flakes can be collected and used for another project.

5 Distress the gold with a rag and white (mineral) spirit. Gently rub the gold until the red colour shows through. You can make the effect as gently or heavily distressed as you like by varying the amount of rubbing.

6 Fix the whole surface with a mixture of 175 ml (6 fl oz) transparent polish (shellac) and 50 ml (2 fl oz) methylated spirit (wood alcohol). Apply sparingly in even downward strokes using a polish brush. The polish may appear chalky at first but this will dry clear within minutes. Leave the polish to dry thoroughly, approximately 30 minutes.

7 Decide on a leaf design and trace it onto the gold surface using a hard lead pencil and red chalk pastel.

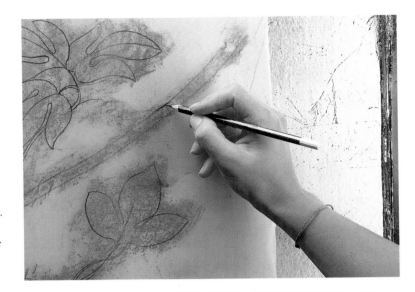

8 Squeeze about 2.5 cm (1 in) each of burnt sienna, black and burnt umber oil colours onto a plate or palette. Pour 50 ml (2 fl oz) gloss varnish into a metal container with an equal amount of white (mineral) spirit. Mix well. Paint on the leaves in a rusty colour using a small sable brush, changing the shade slightly for each leaf.

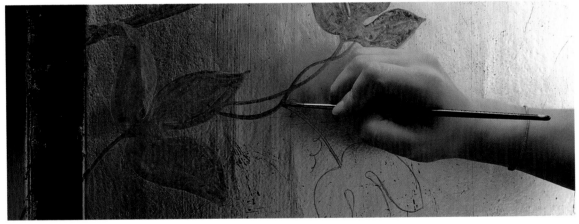

9 After painting a section pat the colour with a clean rag to give it a mottled appearance. This will also help the colour of the leaf show through the paint and will give it a translucent effect. Continue painting and patting until the design is complete. Leave to dry overnight.

10 Pour 175 ml (6 fl oz) gloss varnish and 100 ml (4 fl oz) white (mineral) spirit into a jar or tin. Mix 2.5 cm (1 in) Indian yellow and 1.5 cm (½ in) each of burnt sienna and black oil colours into the varnish mixture. Apply the coloured varnish to the screen using a medium bristle brush, working on one panel at a time, first using vertical and then horizontal strokes so that the varnish is even and covers the whole surface. Work quickly as the varnish has to be softened while still wet.

11 Stipple the badger brush onto the varnish starting from a top corner and working downwards. The brush lines soften out to produce a smooth, even surface. Do not go back onto a section which is tacky as the lines will be made more prominent. If you are not pleased with the result, remove the varnish with white (mineral) spirit and start again. When the screen is finished, leave to dry overnight in a well-ventilated dust-free room.

JARDINIÈRE

SARAH POTTS

THE ART OF TOLEWARE, or painted metal, became popular in the mid-eighteenth century in France and England. The vogue for lacquer was still at its height and the idea of producing beautiful but durable artefacts that could be used around the home caused great excitement. Here red japanning complements the rich metallic colours of the jardinière's decorative motif. Ink-work and shadowing complete the delicate finish.

~

MATERIALS AND EQUIPMENT

• *jardinière or ornamental metal pot* • *soft rags* • *methylated spirit (wood alcohol)* • *metal primer* • *small bristle brush* • *red undercoat* • *medium bristle brush* • *red and black eggshell (semi-gloss) paint* • *gloss varnish* • *white (mineral) spirit* • *crimson lake, black, burnt umber and Indian yellow oil colours* • *badger brush* • *tracing paper* • *hard lead pencil* • *white chalk pastel* • *masking tape* • *small sable brush* • *silver liquid leaf* • *gold liquid leaf* • *transparent polish (shellac)* • *black Indian ink* . . . . . .

1 Clean the surface of the jardinière. Use a rag dampened with methylated spirit (wood alcohol) to remove grease and dirt. Apply a coat of metal primer painting the inside first, brushing in upward strokes with a small bristle brush. Leave to dry according to the manufacturer's instructions.

2 Paint red undercoat onto the outside only, applying it evenly with a medium bristle brush, making sure there are no dribbles. Leave to dry overnight, then apply a coat of red eggshell (semi-gloss) paint to the outside.

3 Mix 60 ml (2½ fl oz) gloss varnish with the same amount of white (mineral) spirit. Mix together 1.5 cm (½ in) each of crimson lake and black oil colour to produce a dark red shade. Mix in well with the varnish solution. Use a small bristle brush to apply the varnish, brushing it on thoroughly and evenly, and then brush it out with a medium bristle brush. Use a badger brush to soften the colour. Gently stipple the wet varnish until it becomes tacky and the surface has an even, rich colour. Leave to dry overnight.

4 Decide on your design and transfer it to tracing paper. Draw over the design on the back using a white chalk pastel. Use some masking tape to keep the tracing steady. Press the pencil firmly to make sure the chalk pastel transfers to the pot.

5 Use a small sable brush to paint the design in silver liquid leaf. Allow to dry for 15–20 minutes, then apply the gold liquid leaf. If there are handles paint these in gold liquid leaf. Apply a second coat of liquid if it has not covered well. Pour a small amount of transparent polish (shellac) into a tin, enough to cover the liquid leaf. Mix into the polish half the amount again of methylated spirit (wood alcohol) to produce a fixing polish and apply with a small sable brush to fix the decoration. Be thorough as liquid runs easily when varnished unless it is fixed well. Apply 2 coats of fixing polish to be sure.

6 Use a small sable brush with a good point to apply the black Indian ink. Brush onto a piece of paper first to remove most of the ink so that you do not have too much on your brush: a minimal amount of ink is needed on the brush to paint on fine lines. The harder the brush is pressed onto the surface the thicker the line, so for really fine lines use the very tip of the sable. Indian ink dries within seconds, so if you make a mistake remove it straight away with a damp rag.

7 Squeeze a little burnt umber and Indian yellow oil colour onto a palette or plate. Mix these colours together using a small sable brush and add a small amount of varnish to produce a warm brown colour for the shadows. Brush on in long flowing strokes to achieve a two-dimensional effect.

8 Pick out the top and bottom edges in gold liquid leaf using a small sable brush. Wait 15-20 minutes and then apply fixing polish. Paint the inside of the pot with black eggshell paint, brushing upwards from the bottom of the jardinière with a medium bristle brush. Clean the top outside edge with a rag to remove any eggshell which may have dripped over. Leave to dry overnight.

9 Pour 60 ml (2½ fl oz) gloss varnish into a tin, then add the same amount of white (mineral) spirit. Mix 1.5 cm (½ in) black with 4 cm (1½ in) burnt umber oil colour to achieve an antique effect. Paint the inside with this shade, first brushing it on with a small bristle brush, then brushing it out evenly with a dry medium bristle brush. Apply the coloured varnish to the outside in the same way, making sure you brush from the bottom upwards to avoid dribbles of varnish on the inside. Leave to dry overnight in a well-ventilated dust-free room.

SUPPLIERS

BARCLAY LEAF IMPORTS, INC., 21 Wilson Terrace, Elizabeth, New Jersey 07208; telephone: (908) 353-5522. Gold leaf and gilding supplies.

EASY LEAF, 947 North Cole Avenue, Los Angeles, California 90038; telephone: (213) 469-0856. All types of gold and metal leaf as well as tools and accessories.

SEPP LEAF (FORMERLY GOLD LEAF), 381 Park Avenue South, New York, New York 10016; telephone: (212) 683-2840. Metal leaf, gilding supplies.

REED'S GOLD LEAF, P.O. Box 160146, Nashville, Tennessee 37216; telephone: (615) 865-2666. Gilding equipment, books, and videos.

ACKNOWLEDGEMENTS

Thank you to everyone who has helped and supported us in producing this book. A special thank you to 'Salvo' who has taught everyone who has worked at Titian's with enthusiasm and patience, and to John Allsop Antiques for the loan of the photographs on pages 6 & 9. The knowledge and love of our work is due to Papa. A big thank you also to Amanda for all the help given at short notice and to James Glancy for all his work and friendship.

INDEX